Praise for
From All Sides

"I recommend this exceptional book to both those interviewing for a job and those conducting the interview. It covers the field of knowledge in recruiting but has a wonderfully rich content that goes further than most because the theory is amplified by a myriad of real-world examples and practical experience."

—**John Goody,**
Vice Chairman (Retired), Marmon Holdings Inc.,
A Berkshire Hathaway Company

"Learn from an expert like Al Polson. He shows how to find, recruit, and shape the best employees for your company. On the other hand, if you are looking for a job, Al reveals the secrets to getting hired. The interview skills he describes will last you a lifetime."

—**Blythe McGarvie, Best-Selling Author of *Shaking the Globe: Courageous Decision-Making in a Changing World*, Three-Time Recognition as One of the "Most Influential People on Corporate Governance and in the Boardroom," NACD/Directorship**

"In a thought-provoking, clever style, Mr. Polson takes you behind the scenes of the professional recruiting world. *From All Sides* provides plenty of down-to-earth details that would be helpful for those contemplating a career in management or human resources. In addition, it lays out invaluable tips and ideas for anyone who is thinking of interviewing for a first job or new position. Mr. Polson is a shrewd and funny chronicler, toggling beautifully between personal experience and relatable methods that can make a positive difference in a successful candidate or hire. This book has a keen sense of balance and analysis. As a retired executive with extensive experience in staffing and recruitment, I highly recommend *From All Sides* to any person looking to improve their knowledge of how to be the best hiring manager or candidate in this competitive job market."

—**Diane Dunlap, EVP, Chief Administrative Officer,**
Bank Administration Institute

"*From All Sides* is an exceptional book that combines humor, wisdom, and a unique perspective on the recruitment process. Al Polson's ability to bring levity to a topic often seen as dry and mundane is truly commendable. Whether you're a job seeker, a recruiter, or an employer, this book is a must-read that will leave you with valuable insights and a smile on your face."

**—Dr. James R. Gregory,
Chairman Emeritus, Tenet Partners,
and Bestselling Author of *Fortune Teller***

"Al Polson's book, *From All Sides*, is essentially a guide or handbook to be followed by successful job seekers, recruiters identifying and vetting candidates for corporate jobs, hiring managers within corporations, and even corporate executives. *From All Sides* should be used as a primer in college business schools across America. Very little attention is often paid by these schools to the hiring process used today by American corporations."

—Emery Conyers, PhD, MBA

"Al Polson's *From All Sides* is a must-read guide for hiring managers, business owners, and executives alike. It is educational and entertaining, as well as informative and very interesting."

—Bill Chronert, President of Pacific Funding

"Al is a font of wit and wisdom. He combines both in his reflections on recruiting and advice for capitalizing on all angles of the hiring process. *From All Sides* brings value for hiring managers, candidates, and recruiters in an enjoyable read."

—Len Norman, President of The Colonial Group

"Al Polson's book, *From All Sides*, is an extremely powerful look into the world of finding employment and recruiting. It gives a candid perspective on the inner workings of corporate recruitment practices and why companies may struggle to identify top talent. Furthermore, it frames the intricate balance between the roles of recruiter, individual job seeker, and corporate HR environments. Al delves into his personal philosophies and practices that enabled him to build one of the most successful recruiting agencies in America. Based on his extensive experience as a senior corporate leader to starting his own firm, Al unpacks the complexities that can lead to ineffective decision-making in the corporate setting and the potential frustrations that candidates may inadvertently create for themselves.

In his characteristic laid-back style, Al presents a unique view from all sides, offering insight and practical advice to both corporate HR teams and individuals searching for that next great position. It's a must-read book for anyone working their way through the hiring process."

—**Dr. Steven Brown**

"*From All Sides* is a must-read for job applicants, hiring managers, and recruiters. Mr. Polson has taken his forty-five-plus years in both the corporate and recruitment arenas and provided an in-depth and insightful examination of what makes the hiring process successful for all concerned. He does this with candor and a dose of humor. A great read."

—**Stephen McGuffin, Vice President (Retired)**
Wyeth Pharmaceuticals

"In Al Polson's book, *From All Sides*, the author demonstrates his knowledge through his unique in-depth expertise and managerial experience. It explains what is important for both candidates and management during the hiring process in a very clear and concise way. Mr. Polson's techniques of recruiting and the importance of candidate preparedness are invaluable in today's business world. The humor in the "Can't Make This Up" chapter just adds to the readers' enjoyment."

—**John Dunlap, Executive Vice President, Chief**
Operating Officer, United Equitable Insurance Group

"An insider's guide to what goes on behind the scenes in the hiring process from an HR professional. It provides a 360 view of actionable insights for the candidate to hiring manager to the leadership team to make the process more efficient and effective."

—**Bill Canady, Author of *The 80/20 CEO: Take**
Command of Your Business in 100 Days*

From All Sides:
The Truth about the Hiring Process in America

by Al Polson

© Copyright 2024 Al Polson

ISBN 979-8-88824-331-2

All rights reserved. No part of this publication may be reproduced, stored in a retrieval system, or transmitted in any form or by any means—electronic, mechanical, photocopy, recording, or any other—except for brief quotations in printed reviews, without the prior written permission of the author.

Published by

◂köehlerbooks™

3705 Shore Drive
Virginia Beach, VA 23455
800-435-4811
www.koehlerbooks.com

From All Sides
The Truth about the Hiring Process in America

FROM ALL SIDES

The Truth about the Hiring Process in America

AL POLSON

VIRGINIA BEACH
CAPE CHARLES

This book is dedicated to my loving wife, Vicki,
and my two sons, Chris and Matthew.

When I made the crazy decision to leave the comfort and safety
of the corporate world to start my own recruiting company, it
was because of their total support and love
that I could make it a reality.

TABLE OF CONTENTS

AUTHOR'S NOTE 5
BACKGROUND 7
MY OWN INTERVIEWS 11
RECRUITING 101 16
YOU CAN'T MAKE THIS UP 27
LESSONS LEARNED FOR CANDIDATES 42
LESSONS LEARNED FOR HIRING MANAGERS 54
MY HIRING PHILOSOPHY 71
SUMMATION 84
ACKNOWLEDGMENTS 87

AUTHOR'S NOTE

This book is intended to help those searching for a new position or career path. It is also intended to help all companies and their hiring managers working to fill critical positions. Stories of successes and failures are meant to help guide others in their quest for the next great job or hire.

BACKGROUND

In the United States of America, people often ask, how can there be such high levels of unemployment?

With so much wealth, so many companies, and so many jobs, how is it possible? It just can't be so. Well, we are going to look deeply into this supposed phenomenon to see exactly why it is so. What causes it, who causes it, where does it exist, and where does it not? I will try to educate, enlighten, and amuse you with the unbelievable, ridiculous, thought-provoking realities that exist within the employment ranks in this great country.

Having been on all sides now, it is clear to me why people are unemployed and why so many are troubled about it all. I am a firm believer that if we don't laugh at ourselves, we are missing a great opportunity to see things in a more fun-filled and positive perspective, or we simply don't get it. By seeing or attempting to see the funny side of more serious issues, we miss the point. At no time in this book are any of the amusing stories meant to hurt anyone's feelings or make fun of those that are, shall we say, a few bricks short of a load, but if doing so wakes up all the rest, then it is for a good cause.

You see, I spent many, many years in the corporate world. I did so for many years as one of those millions of workers trying to get ahead in the business world with all the "things" that get in the way. We all know those things as politics, the boss's relatives, friends, corporate structures, policies and procedures, the endless supply of theories, bad managers, Peter principle candidates, and so on. In other words, all the "crap" that exists in Corporate America.

People who have not been there or people who have never been exposed to such things have no idea what really goes on. Therefore, a portion of this book is dedicated to hopefully opening many eyes to the realities that exist right under executive management's noses. Some of it is totally unknown to them, although I can't imagine how. They condone some of it to elevate their status even further in their own minds. And yet some of it clearly exists *only* because it is how it has always been. You will grow to see how much I truly dislike that reason even more than the others.

Another portion of this book will be dedicated to the recruiting world of which I am now a member. Or *was* a part of for twenty-one years. I recently retired. After so many years of the corporate world, I started my own business. I tried for years to think of what I could possibly do on my own that would enable me the opportunity to earn a good living and enjoy what I do. So many people have that same dream, yet so few get the chance to fulfill it. I have done it, and I have learned so much about the American workforce, the things people see themselves qualified to do, and how they go about trying to get there. In the stories related to this topic, I think you will be amazed and shocked by the things that go on every day. I still remain shocked almost daily.

Any book worth the price on the back cover will point out all these things to be viewed as wrong or holding us back and *must* offer some solutions. The last portion of the book will attempt to offer some solutions and insights into a better way. Some are very successful ways adopted by others in their organizations or personal approaches, and others are my personal ideas about how I think things should be done. I developed these ideas based on what I have seen, what I have experienced, what I have been taught, the way I was raised, and more. Hopefully, you will be able to take something from these pages to improve your company's hiring process, your own approach to finding that better job, or your overall view of the world and all the great people in it. Or open your eyes to the stark realities in the real world of dealing with and hiring people.

Everything you will read here is one-hundred-percent true. I will keep the company names confidential, as well as the candidate's names, of course. There was an old TV series called *Dragnet* about two police officers in Los Angeles. They started every show with, "The names were changed to protect the innocent." I am doing somewhat the same thing, but in this case, it is to protect the crazy, strange, sad, totally bizarre, just plain stupid, and, well, yes, even some innocent.

I will start with a background of my own interview experiences in college and during personal job searches. I learned a great deal from those experiences, or so I thought. But *wow*, were my eyes opened wide when I became the interviewer!

After that, I will cover many of the less bizarre interview situations—but just as important—from a lesson-learned perspective. These are all from my twenty-plus years as an executive recruiter. During that time, along with my many years in Corporate America, I have interviewed literally thousands of people. The things that are said and not said have taught me so much about the job-hunting world. There are also those "wish they hadn't said" things that are learning experiences for us all. Then, I will get into some of the unbelievable and true things I have seen and heard with my own eyes and ears that I simply call, "You can't make this up."

Lastly, I want to finish with a summary of important lessons. These are lessons for those of you who are searching for your next career or certainly will be in the future. After all, the average person will change jobs seven times in their career.

Maybe even more important are the lessons I have learned and want to convey to those tens of thousands of corporations that are hiring now or in the future. So many companies make so many mistakes when it comes to their hiring. Most will never admit this because they feel as though their hiring practices are "state of the art" with their own processes, their own recruiting staff, their own personality tests for applicants, and exhaustive interview experiences that seem to be so extensive that they wind up targeting the "last one standing" rather than the *best candidate*! I would love nothing more than to be able to show many of those companies (that don't think they have a problem) why what they are doing could be changed into a more positive experience and successful one.

I will tell this story with vignettes and scenarios that, again, are real and hopefully will get the critical points across. I hope you enjoy!

MY OWN INTERVIEWS

I had a very wise professor in college who told me in my junior year that when companies come to campus to interview juniors and seniors, I should sign up for as many as my schedule would allow. I asked him, "Why would I possibly interview with some of these firms when I have zero interest in pursuing a career there?" He told me that the experience I would gain from each interview would be priceless. He said, someday, those experiences will give me an opportunity to not only get comfortable with the whole process but also to give me the skill sets that will follow me throughout my career. He also said I will begin to see what the interviewer sees, think what they think, and know exactly what they are looking for before they even ask their questions.

Little did I know that later in my career, interviewing would become so crucial to my success. Yes, it allowed me to get certain jobs I wanted over the years, but more importantly, it actually created a whole new career for me later on.

I began taking every interview that came along. I interviewed with large manufacturers, retail stores, service companies, and even law enforcement. It became fun for me. By the time I was finished with my junior year, I knew as much as the interviewers about what they wanted to hear, what they were going to ask, and how I did. Some I didn't do so well; some I aced. In every case, though, I learned something I could take with me.

In all these college interviews, I learned the art of BS. By that, I mean the skill of answering the "blue sky" questions. The hiring world is so often wrapped up in the "behavioral-based questions" to test your "situational awareness" that they forget to ask the basics about the job. You know what I mean if you have ever been in an interview. Such as, "Tell me about a time you had to work for or with someone who was difficult." Or "Tell me about a time when you had to create a new product or idea from scratch." Or how about the questions related to the bizarre, such as, "Tell me how you would handle this," and then they give you a situation that has about the same relevance to a job that your high school trigonometry class did?

Don't get me wrong; many behavioral-based questions are very good at analyzing your ability to think on your feet and gauge how you handle certain situations. But some of them have zero relevance to the job or even the company culture. We will get into company culture later, but it is one of the *most* important aspects of a job and interviewing for that job, and yet so little time is spent on discussing it.

Let me give you an example of behavioral-based questioning that meets my description of bizarre and, frankly, a total waste of time. Maybe then you will see why I think this area of interviewing can go too far.

Midway through my career, I managed a large purchasing department. At the time, I had roughly fifteen-plus years of experience and some rather large accomplishments. Some of those had been written up in national papers, etc. I led a team that put together one of the first outsourcing projects in the world. As such, we had the potential to save millions of dollars. This is not boasting; it is simply a fact that came about through a great team of people working with me. It was definitely a team effort I happened to lead.

In any case, as most people do at some point, I got bored and started to just "nose" around to see what other opportunities were out there. I received a call from the vice president of a major credit card company that employed tens of thousands of people. He told me he had some major issues with his large purchasing group, and he had been hearing and reading about some of the things we had accomplished. He asked me to come in for an interview so he and I could sit down and discuss what I could do to improve his operation. He said the caveat was that the company policy was to come in for an all-day interview and testing. After that, we would sit down and go over the details of the job.

I had no idea what I was in for. First of all, I took a test that made the SATs look like a pop quiz. The questions had nothing to do with purchasing or, for that matter, the company I was interviewing with. They gave me two hours to take it. I finished in about an hour and forty minutes. I gave the test to the person monitoring me and said I was done. She actually said, "Are you sure? We have never had anyone finish it before."

I figured right there and then that I had sent up a "red flag" because I was out of the norm. That meant I had either done a great job with it or totally missed the mark on what they were asking. Either way, at that point, I had a bad feeling.

The next step was to have a series of panel interviews and some "situational awareness" meetings. In comes a couple of people, probably in their early twenties. At most, maybe. Now, don't get me wrong; most of the people I have hired are young people, so this is not about age. But it is about knowing the real world. They proceeded to lay out a scenario about credit cards and credit card holders, what they wanted in their cards, and so on and so on. Then they gave me a bunch of statistics about credit cards and went through a series of questions that had *no bearing* on why I was there. They wanted me to do some calculations and devise a solution to their problems with their credit cards and why their customers would shop for different cards. The whole thing made no sense. People shop for credit cards because of the benefits they get and the interest they are required to pay. Nothing more, nothing less. This was not at all what they wanted to hear. They went into some things, clearly that they had read out of a textbook, and said for me to relook at it all based on that. I finally said, "Let's wait a minute" (and this is where I lost them and, thankfully, the job). I said, "Do you folks know why I am here?" They said, "Sir, it doesn't matter what job you are here to interview for; everyone needs to be able to solve these behavioral questions to our satisfaction."

Now, keep in mind, *they called me for help*. Or at least the vice president did. So, I told them I didn't understand the relevance of the questioning, and frankly, it made no sense in the scheme of things. The next group came in, and there was more of the same. Then the last group came in, and they were all subordinates of the position I was there to talk about. After about fifteen minutes of that meeting, I knew why the vice president had called me. He had some major problems. Now, if you were a subordinate and you had a chance to interview your future boss or boss's boss, would you want someone that everyone knew was going to come in and clean the house? Especially if their résumé indicated that they knew what they were doing and had done so in the past with great success? I don't think so. Subordinate interviews are a good idea if handled properly and if the results are reviewed in context.

Finally, I met briefly with the VP, and he asked how it went. I told him I greatly appreciated the opportunity, and I knew I could do a great deal to help him, but I am certain the interview group would not approve. I also told him they really need to take a look at their process and tailor each interview to more specific scenarios related to the job. He totally understood and said he agreed. But now, get this, he said he could not overrule the twenty-year-olds . . . even for his own direct hires.

Do you see something wrong with their process?

One of the *key* elements of interviewing I learned was that no matter what, answer with your true feelings. Show the interviewer your passion for the job and, frankly, your passion for life. By this, I mean let them see you and your true self. If you want the job, I mean *really* want the job, *tell them*. Don't say it in a way that sounds like you are begging and desperate for it. But let them know this is something you believe in, something you feel strongly about, that you can make a positive difference in their company.

My father always taught me these things, and he taught me to *do the right thing*. His favorite saying was, "Once a task is begun, never leave it until it is done. Be it great or be it small, do it right or not at all."

That stuck with me and still sticks with me. I actually told these things to key people I interviewed over the years because I believed in it, and I also thought it said a lot about who I believed I was.

On at least three occasions while interviewing for a job I really wanted, I told the story about what my dad taught me. At the end of the interviews, as they so often do, they ended their portion by asking, "Are there any other questions you would like to ask?" On all three of those interviews, I said, "Yes, I would like to ask you if there is anything else I can answer for you, to prove to you that I am the person for this job?"

I got all three jobs.

Also, intermingled throughout the book are what I call motivational words of wisdom that I wrote over the years to help inspire my team. Recruiting is a tough business, and there are lots of ups and downs. So, I have always felt a team needs occasional words of encouragement and positivity to get through those downs.

RECRUITING 101

After spending the last twenty-plus years in recruiting, I can safely say it is the one business on earth—that I am aware of—that teaches you more about human nature than any other profession. I have always told my prospective new hires that they will learn more about people (good and bad) than they ever thought possible. I also always tell them that after doing this for a few years, their friends and others they meet will never truly read people the way they can.

None of them believed me, but man, do they all believe me now!

This business will either make you tough and smarter about fellow human beings, or it'll make you run for cover.

Let's face it, people are odd characters. Many will do and say almost anything to get a job or advance a career. They will lie. They will cheat. They will say yes and really mean no. They will not communicate with you. Heck, they won't even communicate with their significant other. They will ask the dumbest questions ever. They will overanalyze, underestimate, exaggerate, and do things so crazy that you wouldn't ever suspect it.

However, many are as kind, nice, and honest as can be. Many will be brutally honest about their abilities, needs, goals, etc.

Both of these descriptions can be said of candidates, but just as much can be said of interviewers, hiring managers, and executives.

We, as recruiters, can see the absolute highs of highs and the lows of lows during any given day. Heck, we can see those things in any given hour. The person who we can help get their dream job, the job of a lifetime, can be the ultimate high. Then, the very next call can be from a hiring manager who says the person who was supposed to start work never showed up or called. Thus is the recruiting business.

Why would anyone do this, you ask? I have often asked myself that—sometimes multiple times in the same day!

The truth of the matter is that it can be the best job in the world. That is, if you do it right, believe in what you are doing, love the idea of changing a person's life with a job that gives them everything they have ever wanted, like helping a struggling company fill a needed position, are willing to accept the good and bad in life with the understanding that you must move on and learn from each situation, and are tough enough to take those lows and eager enough to win those great wins; if these apply, then you will understand it. People love it or hate it, just like many jobs. But when you are successful and start to *get it*, then it all makes perfect sense. Besides, it pays quite well!

As I have said, I have interviewed hundreds of people. I have been involved in thousands of interviews. Just when I think I have seen it all, something new comes along. Someone does or says something that I didn't think possible. Or a situation develops that seems unlikely or even impossible. But we moved on. Life moves on.

One of the keys to my company was our full-service recruiting approach. By that, I mean we interviewed each candidate before we sent them to a client. Most of the time, we did so at least twice. I don't mean via email or text as many modern-day recruiters do. No, we picked up the phone and had lengthy conversations with them.

We actually had a multistep process that we developed. These many steps attempted to cover every possible aspect considered critical to the hiring process and our client. I won't go into all of the detailed steps here.

We would also verify the details of the résumé. We would then talk to all spouses or significant others when a relocation was involved. We did this not only to offer information on the company and relocation but also to make sure the candidate (their partner) had actually discussed this relocation with them. I know that is shocking to think they wouldn't!

We would check references, professional references, that is, not their minister or high school gym coach. We would also try to find others who could attest to their work and accomplishments because, let's face it, many references are friends from work and will paint a pretty picture.

Our philosophy, quite honestly, was to "do the right thing" and not send a candidate we wouldn't consider hiring ourselves.

I always enjoyed our weekly meetings, where we shared motivational words of wisdom. Many were originals, and that made them even more special. This is one I wrote for my team about what I believe and what we stand for as a company.

DO THE RIGHT THING

You wake up one day and suddenly realize
You don't like what you see before your very eyes.
You know deep down you are a person who is good
But sometimes you don't do things as you should.
You know in your heart the right things to do
But other things not on that list pull at you too.
You understand how people sometimes do wrong
And get pulled down a road that is ugly and long.
However, if you look deep inside and really see clear,
You know that the good in you is very, very near.

So, you dig deep and take a hard look at what you see
And realize you know who you really want to be.
You have to want it more than before.
You have to do the right thing more and more.
When you make this decision, that is the hardest part
Because getting started begins deep in your heart.
Then you are on the road to being the best you can.
It makes you feel so great to finally understand
It feels so great to do things right.
It gives you hope, happiness, and true sight.

Despite all our efforts and best intentions, things do go awry. After all, we are dealing with human beings, right? There are hundreds of situations I could discuss, maybe thousands.

Below are a few examples of real-world situations.

One of the things all recruiters and hiring companies deal with is, quite honestly, lying on a résumé. I could soft-play this and say exaggerations on their résumé. Or mistakes on a résumé. And sometimes that is all it is. However, there are so many examples of outright lying, so it has to be discussed.

There are lies about all kinds of things. For example, many lie or try to mislead about their education. One of the quick ways to pinpoint this misdirection is seeing a college or university with "attended" in the fine print. Now, you might ask, how is this a lie? And it truly isn't a lie if it is clear that they did not graduate. They know the recruiter or hiring manager assumes they got their degree from there. The attentive recruiter or hiring manager will dig deeper and find out if they did. We see this just about every day. In many cases, they never attended that college at all. Or any college, for that matter. They know a degree is required, so education is one of the most abused areas.

Many people, and I mean many, exaggerate various aspects of their experience. They will look at a job posting and try to match, word for word in some cases, the exact terminology that the company is looking for. For example, a job posting for a specific type of engineer, accountant, scientist, you name it. They will list their qualifications as if they were coming right out of the job description.

Detailed questioning about the various tasks can oftentimes "dig out" the "inaccuracies" of the résumé. In taking the time to fully vet the candidates, you can quickly find the ones who

- Said they went to college but didn't.
- Said they had a degree but did not.
- Claimed to be an engineer but could barely spell it.
- Claimed to be an accountant but couldn't even add.
- Said they were managers but never had been.
- Had knowledge of certain scientific data but were not scientists at all.
- Supposedly had knowledge of certain machinery but had never seen it.
- Claimed to have food manufacturing experience but actually just worked at McDonald's.
- Vowed that they were familiar and experienced with processes like just-in-time but were actually never involved.
- Claimed to know robotics but apparently learned from watching *Star Trek*.

The list goes on and on.

For example, I had a great client in the manufacturing industry who had struggled for months to find a specific type of engineer. Unfortunately, their process on this particular job and the particular hiring manager was that they wanted me to submit résumés, and they would vet them. I asked them to please let me vet them and check their references. They indicated that they had a company they paid to do such things, so I relented. I submitted several résumés from my database that seemed to fit the description. This was totally against my philosophy of how I liked to do business, but they were a great client, and I had placed many people with them. For all those other placements, I was allowed to do the reference checks, etc. This job was somehow different, and thus, I was sort of hands-off.

In any case, they hired one of my submittals, and all was well. Or so I thought. They called me *two years later* and told me they didn't think he was an engineer at all, and in fact, they also didn't believe he had a degree. So, I asked why they thought these things, and they said that little hints started becoming clear as they put him on various projects; he didn't seem to understand what to do. But then the kicker came into play. Apparently, this candidate, now an employee, and his wife started having major marital issues. She got angry, called the company, and told one of the executives out of the blue that her husband wasn't who he had said he was—he was not an engineer and didn't have a degree.

Now, remember that he had been in that job for two years! So, they asked me to do the reference checks and verification of education—that I wanted to do from the start. Sure enough, he did not have a degree and had never even attended college.

Can you imagine? He had been "acting" as an engineer for two years! Needless to say, I was allowed to do references and background checks after that.

⬅➡

Most of our jobs involved relocation. Working in more senior-level positions often means a person will have to move to the position. It is just a way of life. Over the years, we have had so many candidates who needed to relocate that we developed the previously mentioned policy of talking to the significant other to help verify that relocation is indeed a real potential. No matter what the candidate says, let's face it, if the spouse isn't going, they are not going.

Talking to significant others proved to be a valuable tool. You would be shocked how many people were job hunting and had never told their spouses. You never know if they are just "kicking tires" to see what is out there or if they are going to tell them after they get an offer. Well, we tried very hard to *never* allow surprises. Thus, the policy was developed.

I had a relatively new employee who forgot this step. They did not speak to the spouse. The candidate went through several interviews, and lo and behold, they got an offer. They accepted the offer. So, my recruiter called to congratulate them, and the wife answered. She was in shock. She had no idea what we were talking about.

I bet that was some conversation later that night! He withdrew from the process. That recruiter never made that mistake again.

⭠⭢

One of the most disappointing things in the recruiting profession is what I will call "the ultimate lie." It is when everything goes great, the candidate does a terrific job, and the client finally gets what they have been searching for. The offer is made; it is a tremendous offer. A life-changing offer, in fact. The candidate accepts the offer, and all is right with the world.

The start date has come, and there is a *no-show*. They don't show up, they don't call, they don't email, and they don't text. They don't answer their phones. They all but disappear.

Then suddenly, you reach them, and they say, "I changed my mind at the last minute," or "I got a counteroffer from my current company and decided to stay."

And you couldn't call me? After all the work we did to get you this opportunity of a lifetime, you couldn't have the decency to call me or the hiring company to let us know? The answer is typically, "Well I knew you would be upset, so I didn't want to call." *Seriously?* There is more at stake here than me being upset. How about the hiring company? How about their plans and training and so on? How about your reputation in the marketplace?

People change their mind, but for goodness's sake, where is the professionalism? Where is the courtesy? Where is the decency?

Apparently, they did not get the same lessons in life that I did. What a horrible way to treat others. I decided to write about that very important belief because it impacts us all every day. I wanted my team to realize that we will treat others the way we want to be treated no matter what they do or say or how they act.

HOW I SEE THE GOLDEN RULE

The Golden Rule is special to me.
I was taught early that it's a gift that is free.
To care about others the way you should
Even when someone else never would.
Do unto others as you would have them do unto you.
Treat others the way you want to be treated.
Think about others before you think of yourself.
Always take other people's feelings into consideration before your own.
No matter how we say these words, the same thing is true.
You should always think about others before you think of you.
If you keep this thought in mind every single day,
In the long run of life, you will feel it surely pay.
We try to do these things with all that we meet.
Considering some of the folks, it is not an easy feat.
But I believe it is what keeps them all coming back
Because we treat them all with kindness and tact.

Our success is here for a reason, and that much is true.
Let's keep it that way forever in all we say and do.
The Golden Rule here lives strong and bright.
It will always be so because we do what is right.

We constantly had folks that changed their minds or received counteroffers. I understand that. It happens. But please communicate those decisions with the right people.

A quick point on counteroffers. People decide to leave a company for various reasons. It can be compensation, location, company culture, the hiring manager, or the actual day-to-day work.

If you have made the decision to leave, there is something pushing you to do so. Whatever the reason, it was meaningful enough to cause you to take a serious step forward in your career. So, you start looking, and you find exactly what you were looking for. In fact, you find the very things that were missing from your other job.

So, you accept another offer, which supposedly fills all the missing parts from your existing job. You let your current employer know by giving notice. Suddenly, they come back to you with an offer for more money. Sometimes, large amounts of money. You feel honored and cherished. Should you?

You were leaving the job for a reason, or maybe many reasons. Now that you are leaving, your company realized your true worth out of the blue. Why now? Why so much? Is it because you are worth it, or is it because they are trying to risk losing you in the short term and having a void they can't afford at this point in time?

Many companies make a counteroffer for one simple reason. They can't afford to lose a key person here and now. So, they "throw money at you" to keep that from happening. However, just as many will start to look for a replacement in the long run.

Why? Because you have shown you are ready to leave, and like it or not, loyalties are broken. There are all kinds of statistics out there about this subject. One such statistic is that 80 percent of people who accept a counteroffer are not at that company by the end of the next twelve months. Now, I don't know if that number is true, but I can't tell you how many folks we have seen get the counteroffer, take it, and months later call us again to help them find another job. It happens all the time.

If you get a counteroffer, ask yourself one thing. *Is the extra money going to change the things that caused me to look in the first place?* If the only reason was money, maybe it will. If there were other reasons, the answer is most likely no.

I have mentioned many of the negative things that have happened in the recruiting industry. Never fear; we have just as many positives. Like the many, many people who accept a job we found for them and are still with the company years later and have been promoted over and over. They call us as hiring managers to find candidates for their own department.

Or the candidates who accept a new job and send thank-you notes, flowers, or candy and tell us how much of a positive impact we have had on their families and lives.

Or spouses who call and thank us for the new life they have and for helping to make their spouse the happiest they have been in their lives.

These stories are plentiful and wonderful. Even those folks who did not get the job they were hoping for thanked us for how professionally we treated them and how thorough we were in the process. They continue to stay in touch for years to come, and in many cases, we do ultimately find them that dream job.

⬅➡

This may not sound like a positive story, but in many ways it is. Many of our jobs at the senior level require a physical. We had a fantastic candidate who was also a very good person. He accepted an offer for a great job. There was the requirement of a physical before starting work. He called us a week later and told us that the physical showed that he had advanced cancer, which he had no idea about. The doctors told him that he did not have long to live.

How is this positive? It is a tragedy. He thanked us for the work we did and for the fact that there was a physical. Without it, he would have never known and would not have gotten to spend time with his loved ones and say his proper goodbyes. Heartbreaking. We were blown away by all of this, and even to this day, I still remember his words. What a special man.

YOU CAN'T MAKE THIS UP

One of the best parts of the recruiting business is dealing with all types of people—people from all walks of life, with all kinds of views and backgrounds, who see and do things, let's just say, a little differently. In this section, I will tell you about numerous real-life situations that are too bizarre and actually too funny, in some cases, to have made up. These are all true.

Before starting my recruiting company, I worked for twenty-five years in the corporate world. Obviously, I interviewed hundreds over that time period, with many crazy stories. In one of my positions, I was the director of outsourcing for a major company. I needed to hire several project managers for the various companies we were going into. My direct report and I had set up dozens of interviews in each city. We would book a hotel room with a suite for the interviews. He and I knew we had some long days ahead, so we decided it was best not to waste time if the candidates were clearly not going to be a fit. So, he said, let's have a signal to let each other know. He said, "I will stand up and say, 'Would you like some coffee or water?' Then you will know I feel this candidate is not what we are looking for." I said, "Okay, and if I agree, I will say, 'Yes, please. I would like some coffee,' and if I disagree, I will say, 'No thanks.'"

So, he was going to take the lead and initiate the signal. I had known him for nearly twenty years, so I knew we would see things the same way most of the time. The first gentleman shows up, and he looks totally scared out of his mind. I don't mean nervous. I mean, literally frightened. Remember that this interview is for a project manager to lead a large group of people.

We had arranged the three chairs in a circle so everyone was on equal footing and the candidates could see each of us without difficulty. He took his seat and clenched onto the arms of the chair as if he were going to fall out if he hadn't. He stared at the floor, and no matter what we said, he would not look up. Not once. Frankly, I was starting to worry about the guy, thinking he would pass out. About that time, Mark, my teammate, stood up and said his line. I said, "*By all means!*" Needless to say, that didn't go on much longer.

The next few interviews went well, and we had some good prospects. It had started to snow, and our suite had large floor-to-ceiling windows. So, the next lady came in for her interview. She suddenly stood up, walked over to the window, and said, "Aren't the snowflakes lovely? I like to look at each of them individually." Even though Mark was to take the lead, I jumped out of my seat and said, "I am getting some coffee *now*!" Again, that one ended quickly.

During my recruiting days, I was conducting interviews for a recruiter position within my own company. As I always do, I get passionate about my company. In doing so, I talk about all the things we do for our employees. There is a great deal of training, shadowing with other employees, multiple chances for feedback, etc. I then get into the numerous rewards for hitting our daily, weekly, monthly, quarterly, and annual goals. I will detail those rewards, including a possible trip for the employee and a guest to Las Vegas for hitting the yearly goals. In addition, there are several monetary rewards, commissions, and bonuses. I go into all of that with a great deal of positivity and excitement. I was doing this with a specific candidate, and after my talk of about twenty minutes, I always like to ask, "Before we get into the details of the job and day-to-day duties, do you have any questions so far?" She said, "Yes, how much time off do I get?"

Now, maybe it is just me and my old-fashioned beliefs, but I was taken aback. After all I had just described, pouring my heart out about my company, that was all she cared about? So, I said, "Seriously, after all I just went into about the company, the rewards, and the goals, that is your first question?" She said, "Yes, that is all I really care about." I simply said, "You can have all the time off you want because it won't be here." I ended the interview.

I was interviewing another candidate for a recruiter position in my other location. This one took even less time. I started my usual spiel, and she interrupted me and said, "It sounds like this is a full-time position to me." I said, "Yes, as spelled out in my job posting, it is a full-time permanent position." She stood up and said, "That is not fair; I don't want to come into an office every day!" She proceeded to storm out and slam the door behind her.

Clearly, not everyone makes it to an interview. Some I wish I had never heard from at all!

One of my recruiters was talking to a potential candidate for a manufacturing job, and it appeared he met the requirements we were looking for. She noticed that he kept trying to be "extra" friendly on the phone call. Unfortunately, this happens from time to time. People flirt, and we train folks to ignore and move on. Or if it gets worse, we tell them to get off the phone and indicate in the notes what that person has done so no others in our office will have to deal with that. She, as she was trained to do, just waved that off and kept her conversation professional. She said it was not a big deal because it was so subtle, and he seemed harmless. She was within earshot of me so I could hear her talking to this guy and asking for his résumé. He said he would send it over.

She got his email within a few minutes, and I heard her gasp. Instead of a résumé, he sent a photo of himself. He was fully nude, standing sideways. He had a cowboy hat, and let's just say, it was not on his head or in his hands. She immediately wrote back to him and told him how inappropriate that was, and we would not be dealing with him in the future. His reply was, "Oh, I thought I had sent my résumé. I must have sent the wrong file." Yeah, right.

Before we send a single résumé to a client, we have done our best to fully identify strengths and weaknesses. Obviously, we match up the key skills to the requirements. But we also try to match personalities to company culture. No matter how hard we try, there are things that simply can't be discovered through detailed questioning. Or things that you would never think to ask. Some things you just take for granted, though. Here are a few examples of what I mean.

I submitted an excellent candidate for an accounting management position to one of my good clients in North Carolina. This guy was good! He had two master's degrees in accounting, one from his home country of Peru and one from a great university in the United States. He spoke eloquently and passed two phone interviews with flying colors. After the second one, the director of HR told me he was outstanding, and the job was his barring some fiasco in the face-to-face interview. I scheduled the interview and told him it would be a panel of three people (a very common practice). I then prepped him on the kind of questions I thought they might ask. I told him how to dress, as we always do. I thought I had covered every possible scenario.

I waited for the call from the HR director on the day of the interview. He called me right after and sounded down. I said, "What is wrong? How did it go?" He said that our candidate walked into the panel interview dressed in a great suit, was very polite, and went up to each of the three interviewers and shook their hands. The third one was a young lady. He shook her hand and proceeded to tell her that she had the cutest dimples he had ever seen. She was so embarrassed that he did that right in front of her peers.

Being a professional, she kept going. One of the first questions was, "Give us an example of how well you work with teams." He answered, "I can work with anyone . . . even women."

When the HR director told me this, I didn't know what to say. So, he said, "I guess that is his South American culture coming out, where they are a little behind the times, and he wanted to demonstrate that he is more than happy to work with women. Obviously, that raised some serious red flags with the team, especially after his comment to the young lady." I said, "This is unbelievable. He went to two universities in the States. There is no excuse, culture or otherwise." He agreed.

I thought I had covered every aspect in his prep, but I didn't think I had to cover something so basic. Who knew?

⬅➡

One of my larger clients was a major coffee manufacturer. Theirs is a household name. I sent a candidate there for an engineering position, and they immediately loved the résumé. He had all the qualifications they were looking for and then some. They did a phone screen, and he passed with flying colors. The next step was a face-to-face at their manufacturing facility.

As we do with all candidates, we fully prepped him. We went over the interview process and coached him the best we could. All was going perfectly.

The morning of the interview, he called me from the company lobby. I immediately panicked, thinking, *What could possibly be wrong already?* He hadn't even started the interview yet. He said, "I can't go through with this." I said, "What do you mean? You are there, and you are fully prepped. You have done everything, and you are ready." He said, "The smell of coffee makes me nauseous." I said, "*What*?" He said, "The smell of coffee makes me sick to my stomach. There is no way I can work in a coffee factory." I said, "How is this possible? We have been talking about this for weeks. We have gone over the company and the job in every detail. You just now have discovered that the smell of coffee makes you sick?" His answer was, "Well, I always knew it, but I thought I could handle it. However, the smell in the factory is obvious." I thought to myself, *NO SH#T!* "Don't you think this is something you should have shared with me? I want you to at least do your best to get through this interview because if you don't, after weeks of discussions and interviews, we are going to look like idiots. Can you do that, or do you think it will be too much?" He said, "I will do my best and give it a shot." I admired him for that, even though I felt foolish.

He went through the interview, and I guess he was a "little off," so they wound up not being interested. For all the millions of coffee lovers out there, this is hard to imagine, but it is what it is.

←→

We sent another candidate to a major pharmaceutical company headquarters for an interview. The interview was scheduled on the tenth floor. Again, we got a call the morning of the interview. The candidate was in a panic. He was in the lobby and said he could not go through with the interview. When we asked why, he said he was afraid of heights. Looking down from the tenth floor freaked him out. I would have never thought of this. Who would?

Honestly, we didn't know what to do other than call the client and explain the issue. They were actually kind enough to move the interview to the first floor, believe it or not. I am not sure why, to be honest, because the job was on one of the higher floors. I guess it was to see what the candidate brought to the table after it had gone that far. Needless to say, that didn't work out.

⇐⇒

My largest client for years was a major manufacturer in North Carolina. They were in the consumer products industry. I recruited for the food industry and the consumer products industry. Many of their requirements are the same, especially regarding research and development. They both have a large need for scientists, product development specialists, chemists, engineers, etc.

The HR director and I had a great working relationship. She and I had worked together for years, and I had placed dozens of very difficult-to-find scientists and chemists. She knew that I understood their needs and the concerns that some candidates place on the industry. As such, we could speak frankly about many things when it came to the talent we were able to provide for them. She would tell me where they fit and where they did not. I would also be frank with her about our candidates and where I felt they were missing skills. However, some of the jobs were so specific and difficult that we had to look past the few missing pieces to truly understand the strengths that outweighed the few weaknesses. That was particularly true of some of the extremely focused development scientists that required a PhD and many years of experience.

The HR director was so nice and had the greatest Southern drawl. When she said my name, Al, it somehow came out to be a multisyllabic word. Al became Aa-el. I always got a kick out of it. That is until the morning of a big interview for a very specialized PhD scientist.

I had worked for months on finding the perfect candidate. I found this woman with tremendous skills and exactly the background we needed. It was the proverbial needle in the haystack that many of these jobs are. It took numerous phone and prep calls to get the candidate ready. PhDs are obviously extremely smart, but they can also be a bit different. Sometimes the smarter and more concentrated their field of expertise, the more eccentric they are. Let's just say that she fit that description.

The HR director called me and said, "Aa-ell!" I notice a much more exaggerated *Al* this time. I knew it wasn't good. She again said, "Aa-el, have you seen this woman?" I said, "No, ma'am, I have not seen her. I have talked to her dozens of times over the last few months, but I have not seen her. Why?" Now, keep in mind that she and I had an honest working relationship, with more frankness than with most other HR folks.

She said, "Aa-el, she is one of the strangest-looking people I have ever seen." I said, "What do you mean?" She said, "Well, her hair is plastered down on her head like it has grease on it, or she has never washed it. Plus, she is in sweats, dirty sweats!" I said, "What do you mean sweats? We spent a good deal of time going over proper interview dress and general interview etiquette." She said, "I know you do. That is why I am so shocked. She has on gray sweats, a gray sweatshirt, and gray sweatpants, and there are food stains all over her shirt. How could anyone come to an interview for a senior-level scientist dressed like that?" Being the good recruiter I am, I said, "Is it possible that she wore that as travel clothes with the intention of changing when she got there?" "No, she didn't bring anything else with her! That is what she intends to wear during this interview. If I introduce her to our VP, he will think I am nuts. But he is really going to think you are nuts for sending her in here!"

Recruiters get blamed for almost everything that can go wrong, no matter how much we prep the candidates. The good news is that my HR director friend would never let me get the blame for something this bizarre; she knew my recruiting process and detailed prep plan.

Smart and eccentric is one thing, but just plain lack of professionalism is another. Dress *does* matter. You get one chance to make that first impression, and that chance dissolves in the old stain on gray sweats. Months of searching down the drain!

I worked with a British firm that was opening a plant in the US. They were successful in Europe and decided to expand to America. The company contacted me and asked me to help them find a plant manager position for their new facility. I was working with the president of the company, and he had given me some detailed ideas of what he was looking for. He felt it would take a special person to lead a brand-new operation with a parent company back in England.

We searched for weeks. We finally found a great candidate who was from a similar industry and had solid leadership skills. He actually seemed excited about working for the British company. Part of the training would be back in England, and he really liked that idea. He had never traveled abroad, and the prospect was a big positive for him. He had read a lot about

England and its history and always wanted to go. Besides all of that, he was a great technical fit.

We submitted the candidate, and they quickly did several phone interviews. They really liked what they heard, and the president was particularly interested in his technical background. So, we set up a face-to-face interview in the States. The company had leased a large facility, and even though the equipment and machinery were not in place yet, they felt it was a good idea to interview in the office they had set up.

The candidate was close enough to drive to the interview. He went into town the night before to be ready for a 9 a.m. interview the next morning. Just a few minutes after 9, my phone rang, and it was the president. That is usually not a good sign. However, in this case, he was laughing his head off. I asked him what the matter was. He said, "You won't believe this, but he came to the interview wearing knickers, a plaid vest, and a bowler hat!" I said, "You are joking!" He said, "No, I am not kidding. I asked him why he was dressed that way, and he said that is how he thought English gentlemen dressed!"

When he told me he had read a lot about England and was fascinated with their culture, I didn't realize his reading was from the early nineteenth century! He literally thought that was how they dressed, and he wanted to impress them with his knowledge.

The president was blown away that he would go to that much trouble. He said it must have taken him a great deal of effort to find the knickers and bowler hat. Instead of being put off by it, he was impressed with his creativity. He really liked the guy, and he hired him almost immediately. It was one of those circumstances that you just can't predict.

⇠⇢

I had a large food company client relatively near my location.

They had requested our help for a maintenance manager role. In food manufacturing, this is a critical role, just as it is in most manufacturing operations. These folks keep their machinery running. It is a specialized position because most of the manufacturers we service utilize very high-speed equipment. If one of those machines goes down, it can mean thousands of dollars a minute in downtime.

So, I worked long and hard to find someone with that type of background. We ultimately did, and the client really liked our candidate. He had all the right experience, and he passed the phone interviews easily. So, I prepped him for his face-to-face interview, going over all the details about the company, its culture, and the usual things. I also went over the proper dress for the interview. Even though on paper this was a maintenance position, it was management, and as such, our client expected people to be in the appropriate business attire for the interview.

Everything was set for the in-person interview on the upcoming Friday. I set up a lunch with the director of HR during the interview since she would speak with my candidate right after lunch. While we were at lunch, her cell phone rang. She apologized and took the call. The look on her face right after told me there was an issue. While talking to whoever was on the call, she said, "He what? He is wearing what?"

Naturally, I couldn't wait to hear this story. As soon as she got off the phone, which didn't take long, she told me the story. She said, "He came into the interview with a Viagra jacket on!" I said, fully flabbergasted, "He did what?" She said again, "He came in with a Viagra jacket on and a pair of jeans." She went on to say, "You know, one of those racing jackets with the large stripe on it and the word VIAGRA spelled out all across the front and back!"

For the first time in a long time, I was speechless. That isn't an easy thing for me. However, trying to be quick-witted, I replied, "I guess he just wanted to show you all he was *up* for the job!" I have no idea where that came from, but it was the first thing I could think of. She let out a huge laugh, and so did I. At least it cut the moment's stress. I said, "I am so sorry. I went over in detail what he should wear, and I have no idea how that is what he chose." As it turned out, one of the key interviewers got called into a plant emergency and was not able to meet with him. So, I went on to say, "If you give him another chance, I will make sure he shows up in a suit." She said, "Okay, I will give him another chance. If he can come in on Monday, we will start over and forget this ever happened."

After lunch, I called him on my way back to the office. I said, "Man, what were you thinking wearing a Viagra jacket into the interview? We went over the interview dress in detail, and this is what you chose?" He said, "I don't have a suit, so I just grabbed the first thing I had." I said, "Here is the deal. They are going to give you another chance if you go in on Monday *wearing a suit*!" I explained how lucky we were that they were going to forget it and start over on Monday. He promised he would go out that evening and buy a suit.

So, Monday came, and as promised, they started from scratch and interviewed him all over. Everyone was able to make the meeting, and it went very well. The next day, the HR director called me with an offer. It was a great offer, and when I called him, he immediately accepted. That is fast and rare, considering the circumstances. All he had to do was take a drug screen, and he could begin work in two weeks. I figured it was a done deal.

That evening, the HR director called me and said, "I have some bad news. He did not pass his drug screen." I said, "You mean he took *that much* Viagra?" She chuckled and said, "No, unfortunately, it was something quite different."

YOU CAN'T MAKE THIS UP!

I could fill volumes with stories like these and more. The fact is, just when you think you have seen it all, something comes along to make you realize *not*! Examples of that come in just about every day of people applying for jobs with backgrounds they think are a match for posted jobs but aren't even close. Now, don't get me wrong; I think people have every right to try and improve their standing in life by reaching for the stars, but let's get serious. For example, these jobs and who applied:

- A director of food and beverage for technical services—the applicant was a cook and landscaper (with a vivid imagination).
- An engineering job—the applicant was a doggie poop patrol person (a real hands-on person).
- CEO position at a food manufacturer—the applicant made hats and shirts (talk about a CEO needing to wear all kinds of hats!).
- A scientific regulatory position—the applicant didn't have transportation but stated they would take a bus if the company would reimburse them. They indicated they could really help the company advance their goals (apparently not so much as to have a ride).
- Sanitation supervisor in a food plant—the applicant had experience cleaning their apartment (but sweeping crumbs from under one's table isn't quite the same).
- Packaging manager at a high-speed pharma company—the applicant worked at a mall clothing store. (I guess the shirts came in a package).
- HR manager position—the applicant was a truck driver. (They do have to handle a wide variety of people).
- Electrical process engineer—the person was a Walmart lawn and garden worker. (There are a lot of things that

need electricity in there!).
- VP of regulatory affairs—the applicant was a stock clerk at Macy's. (I am guessing they had a lot to regulate back there).
- Regulatory affairs scientist—the applicant was in sales at a local office supply store. (You know, those folks you can't ever find when you are looking for something).
- Director of operations for a manufacturer—the applicant was a school bus driver. (I don't know about you, but handling all those kids seems like serious operational skills to me).
- Operations manager—the applicant who applied was a lifeguard.
- Process engineer—a grill cook at Wendy's.
- The applicant said they were applying to any position we had—the reason they applied: they were "contemplating the meaning of life for the last few years because my last employer and I had major differences of opinion."

Of course, there are also those applicants who you just can't help, like the one with twenty-four jobs in the last twenty years. Twenty-four! Or the lady who shows up for the interview with so much perfume on, it literally made the interviewer sick. I know because it was me!

Or the folks who say they are still working for their current employer, but when you call to do a reference check, they haven't worked there in years.

Or the candidates who blame us for not showing up for an interview because we forgot to remind them to bring their insulin. How were we to know they needed insulin? We can't ask about those things.

There are too many to name that indicate they were laid off from their previous job. However, when you dig deep, you learn they were fired. Companies don't typically have a one-person lay off.

I list all these examples not only to demonstrate what really goes on when people are searching for jobs but also to add some humor. Otherwise, if we can't laugh at ourselves and the world around us, we will all go nuts!

LESSONS LEARNED FOR CANDIDATES

There is not a day that I haven't learned something about people. It is one of the key reasons I got into the recruiting field and stayed there for so long. As I have said, it truly is one of the best ways to learn about human behavior.

Yes, I have mentioned a lot of examples of the crazy things that go on in the employment world. After conversing with over ten thousand candidates, placing thousands, and hiring hundreds for my own department or company, I learned a lot of lessons. In over twenty-plus years in recruiting and another twenty-five years of hiring in the corporate world, I feel I can speak with some level of expertise on the dos and don'ts in all areas of job seeking. I would like to offer the key aspects that candidates should focus on as they go forward in their job search.

For the purposes of this book, I will try to limit recommendations. I have volumes of details I could cover, but for now, let's stick to the basics. Follow these, and you will certainly be ahead of most competition.

KNOW YOURSELF
Dig deep within yourself and ask what you are truly looking for. What is it that a company can offer you that you don't already have? What is it that you can offer a company to make it better? What are your strengths and weaknesses? What are your short-

term goals and long-term goals? Formulate responses by asking the question, "Why should they hire me?"

Until you can comfortably answer all these questions, don't consider yourself ready for an interview. You must be prepared to sell yourself to secure a job offer.

> *"When you're prepared, you're more confident.
> When you have a strategy, you're more comfortable."*
> **—FRED COUPLES**

> *"Spectacular achievement is always preceded by spectacular preparation."*
> **—ROBERT SCHULLER**

KNOW THE COMPANY

In today's world of social media and information everywhere, there is no excuse for not doing research on the company you are interviewing with. I cannot count the number of times I have interviewed folks for my own company who have not done that. For one of my first questions, I ask, "Have you had a chance to look at our website to understand a little bit about what we do?" It is amazing how many times that answer is *no*. When I hear that, I don't take the candidate too seriously. Why? If you don't care enough about us—the company you're interviewing with—how can you be serious about the job? And if you are not, why should I be?

When you interview with companies today, they expect you to know about them. In fact, you can bet they are going to ask you about that and why their company is attractive to you. They want to know what it is about them that makes you want to work there. Be ready for it.

TAKE THE PHONE INTERVIEW SERIOUSLY

If you get called for a phone interview, that is great news! The phone interview is the gateway to getting into the company for a face-to-face interview. That is what the job search is all about—getting the chance to meet the hiring team, let them know all about you, and discuss what you bring to the table. It also gives you a chance to ask questions about them.

Normally speaking, though, there is no face-to-face without a successful phone interview. *So, take it seriously*! Prepare for it and clear away all distractions. Make sure there aren't going to be interruptions. Nothing is worse from a hiring manager's perspective than setting aside time for a telephone screen and constantly hearing commotion in the background. I have heard babies crying, dogs barking, and the actual candidate chewing, cooking, or crunching paper. You might as well not bother if you can't have thirty minutes of total silence and concentration.

I even suggest you take the call standing up, walking around while you talk. That causes the body to exude energy and makes you sound more engaged. Take whatever steps are necessary to give the hiring manager the time and focus they need.

- Speak clearly.
- Pay attention to the interviewer's voice patterns and tones.
- Sound upbeat.
- Be conversational.
- Handle any "trick" questions in stride by being alert and thinking on your feet.
- Have notes about areas of interest and possible questions.
- Have your résumé handy.
- Be prepared to answer the salary range question. Most interviewers will not ask this on a telephone screen. However, there are those who do, and often, this stumps

candidates. At this stage, a good answer looks like this: "I am open to discussing that as we move forward in the interview process, and I hear more about the position, and you hear more about me." If that does not close the conversation, and the interviewer pushes for a range, ask them what range they are working in. Normally, they will give that to you, and you can answer that you are comfortable in that range with what you know now.
- → Have a couple of questions ready for them.
- → Don't be afraid to ask for the opportunity to move forward in the interview process. Tell them you are interested in having the opportunity to come in and discuss everything further and meet the team. Even if this job doesn't sound perfect for you, something in their organization may be.
- → End the call by thanking them for their time.

FACE-TO-FACE INTERVIEW

You made it! You reached your goal of getting that face-to-face interview—the opportunity to tell your story and hear theirs, see and understand the environment where you hope to spend the rest of your career, meet your future coworkers, supervisors, and leaders, and better understand what makes them tick.

Are you ready?

There are things you need to do to ensure you are indeed ready. Here is a brief list of things I believe are imperative to getting you off to the right start:

- → Dress appropriately—this does not just mean wearing the proper clothes, although, as we have seen in some previous examples, this is critical. It also means making sure your hair is in place, you are well groomed, (I have to mention this even though it should be obvious), and your fingernails are clean and neat. Make sure, if you

wear perfume, it is just the right amount. Not too much. Shoes should be clean and appropriate.
- Arrive on time—this also cannot be overstated. Nothing will destroy your chances faster than being late for an interview. I always suggest getting to the interview ten to fifteen minutes early. Not too early. Certainly, at least five minutes before at the latest. If you are driving to the interview and are not completely familiar with the area, I suggest driving there the night before to make sure you know where it is. You would be shocked to hear how many people don't do this and get lost and end up late. Yes, I know it is harder to get lost with GPS, but traffic or parking can make a big difference, especially if you are not early.
- Bring certain things with you.
    - A portfolio and two pens so you can take notes. (Invariably, one will stop writing at the precise moment you get there).
    - Several copies of your résumé in case some of the interviewers don't have it.
    - Any notes you may require.
    - A list of questions to ask the interviewers. Be sure to prepare those ahead of time. I suggest ten to twelve. More questions should likely come up as you meet with different folks.
- Firm handshakes and eye contact are important. Smile. Treat every passerby as if they are the company's president. They may be. I have had this happen to me on several occasions. The president will pass by anonymously to see how you handle yourself and treat others.
- Collect business cards from everyone. Thank-you notes to each one later can go a long way.
- Show interest in what they are saying. Don't get too

comfortable in the seat. By that, I mean don't lounge back like it doesn't mean much to you. I have seen this over and over, and it definitely sends the wrong signal.
- Ensure you have stories of experience related to the key points of the job description. Real stories you can speak to so the interviewer can clearly tell you know your stuff.
- At the interview conclusion, don't be afraid to show interest in the job. Ask the interviewer if they feel you have demonstrated the skills and background necessary to qualify you for the position. Reiterate your confidence in your abilities. Ask for the job by making a positive statement about the position. Emphasize it is what you have been looking for and your wish to move forward. Ask when you should expect to hear back.
- End the conversation on a positive note. Thank everyone with a handshake and a smile, and express your interest in the next steps.

The typical (but not always) start of the face-to-face interview is a meeting with human resources. They will review the company and its basic benefits and ask some general questions. These meetings are usually brief, however, necessary. The HR manager will undoubtedly give their opinion of you and how well you did in this meeting, so conduct yourself with confidence and determination.

The second step is usually with the immediate supervisor of the position. This is a great opportunity to ask more detailed questions about the job, the various functions, how the position interacts with other departments, etc. The day-to-day tasks and responsibilities are usually covered here.

Sometimes, there is also a meeting with the peers of the position. These are the folks you would be working with on a daily basis. You will get all kinds of details here. Perhaps some you don't even want! Sometimes peers are reluctant to have someone new, especially if you bring more to the table than they do. Don't take this personally. They likely won't have a large say in who gets hired. However, it is a great opportunity to pick up ideas about the departmental culture. I always suggest caution in peer interviews. Answer their questions and stay on topic. Don't let them pull you astray, talking about the boss or things they do not like. Negativity breeds negativity. You never want to give them the chance to go "running to the boss" about negatives you bring to the table. Use this as your chance to ask questions about the functions of the position. Again, stay on course.

Lastly, there is usually an interview with the overall hiring authority. The person who "signs your paycheck," so to speak. This is most likely a "higher level" of questioning about your background, interests, and long-term goals. This is also where you can get a true picture of the company culture and the inner workings of the overall organization. Have some questions that deal with that culture and his/her outlook for the department. It is a great chance to impress the boss with your overall knowledge and business acumen. Your poise and confidence is critical.

When the interview is over, write a thank-you note to each person you spoke with. Email that to them that evening or the next morning. I have many examples of proper thank-you notes from over the years, but for brevity's sake, make sure you thank them, restate your confidence in your ability to do the job, and say you look forward to hearing from them soon.

Follow up with the hiring manager and HR manager if you have not heard from them in a week or so. This is one of the key steps that candidates often miss. Many feel it is too intrusive. I feel it is quite the opposite. Let them know you are still thinking about this and that you remain interested. Be persistent, but try not to be a pest.

However, I can't tell you how often I have done this, and the hiring manager greatly appreciated the follow-up. They get very busy, and quite often, hiring for this position is not their top priority. It likely is for you, but they may have a hundred things going on. So, reminding them about you and your interest level could make a difference. I know in my own hiring experiences, it has often set an individual apart from the others.

Candidates often ask what types of questions they should ask their potential employer. There are a limitless number of pertinent questions. Clearly, you want to ask those that are most important to you. You also want to ask questions that demonstrate you have given the position and the company a lot of thought. Your questions can lead to building a rapport and establishing a better flow to the conversation. I will review possible interviewer questions in a later section.

Remember, you are not just there for them to determine if you are right for the job. You are also there to determine if the job is right for you. That is why your research prior to the interview is so important. Here are some questions that I always find to be a good start:

- Why is the position open?
- Could you explain the company's organizational structure related to this position?
- How would you describe your management style?
- What specific skills do you see that are most critical to this position?
- Are there particular areas of the department that you are seeking to improve?
- Tell me where you see this department in the next five years.
- What are the basic responsibilities and duties of this position?
- What types of people excel here?

- What goals or objectives do you think need to be achieved in the next three to six months?
- Based on what you know so far, how do you think I would fit into this job and organization?
- If you were to give one piece of wisdom you would want incorporated into this position, what would it be?
- What do you see as the next steps?

Again, there are so many more to ask. Think of what's important to you personally and what demonstrates your knowledge and understanding of the role you are applying for.

You think you have done everything possible, and yet you get the generic rejection letter. Unfortunately, this happens all too often. Why?

KEY REASONS FOR REJECTION

1. **Poor attitude.** Many candidates come across as arrogant. Unfortunately, many employers can come across that way (I will cover this later), but in this case, they can—*you can't*!
2. **Appearance.** Not to "beat a dead horse" here, but many candidates do not think this is that important. *It is!* You get three to five minutes to make that first impression. What they see first sticks. I compare this to a trial lawyer saying things he knows are going to be objected to, but guess what? It is already out there, and you can't take it back. The judge can strike it from the record, but he can't strike it from their memories. The same is true with how you dress and your overall appearance.
3. **Lack of research.** It is obvious to most interviewers when a candidate has not done what they can to learn about the job, company, or industry prior to the interview. This shows an overall lack of interest, laziness,

or arrogance. Do everything you can beforehand to familiarize yourself with any aspect of the company and position that you can.

4. **Not having questions to ask.** Asking good questions shows your interest and demonstrates a solid business acumen. Not doing so can be a big turnoff to prospective employers.

5. **Not being able to answer interviewers' questions.** Anticipate questions. Rehearse your answers. This is especially important regarding questions about your technical knowledge of the job or reasons for leaving other positions. Those two categories are the ones most often missed.

6. **Relying too much on your résumé.** Your résumé should be a paper guide of your background. Employers hire people, not paper. Answering questions by simply restating points on your résumé can send bad signals to an interviewer. Your ability to speak to situations will far outweigh the details of your résumé.

7. **Too much humility.** We are all taught not to brag about ourselves. This is a time to forget all of that. Don't be afraid to describe your accomplishments. You can do it in a way that doesn't sound arrogant. Be prepared to discuss your ability to hit key goals so they can see what you bring to the table.

8. **Not being able to relate your skills to employer needs.** Same as above, however many people slip up when they are unable to completely discuss specifics related to their skill set. This is especially critical for technical jobs such as engineering and research. The employer wants to see that you know what you are talking about. I can't tell you how many times I get calls from the hiring manager after an interview, and they say the

candidate simply could not give enough details to prove they knew the subject matter.

9. **Not being able to handle salary discussions properly.** Let's face it: salary is very important to you. It is also important to the employer. Prepare to discuss your salary and benefit requirements, but do so at the proper time. This is not to be discussed too early. It is usually best to have the employer bring it up. It is also a deal killer if you ask for a ridiculous salary. It can also kill the deal to ask for too little. Be prepared to say you are open to discuss what is appropriate for the position and responsibilities. When they ask what you are currently making, tell them. Do not exaggerate. These numbers are verifiable. Tell them one of the reasons you are seeking another opportunity is for growth in responsibilities and correlated compensation.

10. **Lack of career direction.** Know where you want to go with your career. This should be done well before you get to this point. However, be able to discuss it in a way that relates to the position you are interviewing for. Not knowing what you want or where you want to go wastes everyone's time.

If you are successful in your interview and you get that "job of a lifetime," my heartfelt congratulations to you. Many do. Many thank us over and over for that and for preparing them so thoroughly for their interview. Those are extremely gratifying moments for everyone involved.

Unfortunately, many don't get the job. Take those small defeats in stride. That is all they are—small defeats. You may have lost that battle, but in the long run, you will win the war. What are the takeaways from each interview that does not end in an offer? What did you learn? What can you improve on? What did you do a great job on? Was it the job you really wanted after all? Most importantly, what will you do next time to ensure more success? Were you truly prepared?

I see it so often. A candidate misses out on the "job of a lifetime," at least in their initial opinion, only to find the "perfect" one later. It all starts within yourself. It all starts with what you know to be the "right thing" for you and your family.

"For last year's words belong to last year's language
And next year's words await another voice.
And to make an end is to make a beginning."
—T.S. ELIOT

LESSONS LEARNED FOR HIRING MANAGERS

Yes, hiring managers make just as many mistakes and have just as much room for improvement as candidates. There is a huge difference, though. When a candidate makes a mistake, isn't prepared, or doesn't say the right thing, it costs *them* a job.

When a hiring manager makes mistakes, isn't prepared, or says the wrong thing, it could possibly cost the company numerous great hires. That one fact alone can cause Corporate America to lose money. Plain and simple, not hiring the right folks or losing great folks can cost companies money. In many cases, it can cost millions of dollars a year.

If I could have one wish that I believe would impact the job market and hiring in the United States the most, it would be to train hiring managers across the country on proper hiring practices and interview skills.

I can tell you from firsthand experience that most are not trained in these things. I have trained a lot of people in my career. In addition to training people in the corporate world and my own company for the last twenty years, I was also an adjunct professor at the University of Virginia for many years. I taught all sorts of subjects and have trained all levels of employees. However, the most surprised I have ever been for over forty-five years is when I have had the opportunity to train hiring managers. Some of that has been very informal training over a series of phone calls, and some has been more formal in a classroom-type environment.

I am always shocked by just how little they have been trained on hiring practices and interviewing. And this goes all the way up to senior-level managers. I have seen vice presidents and company presidents in interviews and am blown away by how they conduct themselves and the questions they ask. Sometimes it feels like the higher a person grows in an organization, the more bizarre their interview skills become. I don't know if that is due to their increased comfort level within the organization or a power play, but I know it costs a great deal in the long run.

How is it possible that these poor hiring practices could cost a company millions?

⇐⇒

I have seen this realized over and over. For example, the company needs a senior-level controller or CFO. A candidate comes in with tremendous skills and a strong background in saving their companies millions of dollars. And these are verified accomplishments! Yet the hiring manager, in this case a president, comes across as an arrogant leader (I am using a much nicer sequence of words here, but you can choose your own). He spends the entire interview bragging about himself and his personal accomplishments, which have nothing to do with the company's financial issues.

Of course, the candidate is interested in discussing how they feel hiring them can help turn things around but obviously doesn't want to ignore the president's tales. So, they listen and try to interject financial facts that should be of great interest to the president. Well, the president apparently reads this as being disinterested in his personal accomplishments and ignores the candidate's strengths. He decides this is not a person he would want working for him because the candidate would not want to take his direction. The truth is that the president wanted to surround himself with "yes" men who would sit all day and listen to his stories of personal glory rather than cure the ills of the organization.

This actually happened over and over on numerous types of jobs. Jobs in engineering, research, and sales. It happened in sales positions several times. One thing that can definitely impact a company's bottom line faster than anything is hiring (or not hiring) a great sales leader. A great salesperson can come in and make an immediate impact. I have seen them enter an organization and literally increase sales by millions in the first year due to their connections and people skills.

I recruited numerous sales positions for this same president. At the time, the average recruiter would send twelve candidates for a job before one was selected. At that same time, my average across the country while recruiting for food manufacturing was a three-to-one ratio. I attribute that to my team doing such great research and due diligence on every candidate, so we were able to cut hiring time by 75 percent. Not to mention a drastic reduction in time spent hiring teams for our clients.

I was called in to work on a senior sales position for this president. Our database was full of great candidates who met and exceeded the requirements. Or so I thought. To make a very long story short, I wound up submitting thirty-five candidates before I had to throw up my hands and quit. Yes, I quit the client. I could not afford to waste any more of my team's time. These candidates were all thoroughly researched, vetted, and interviewed before sending them.

What we couldn't know is that they were being turned down because he didn't like the school they went to, they didn't love his stories, or they didn't seem like "yes" people. Who knows? It could have been that he didn't like how they combed their hair! We know that after each batch of candidates we sent, he decided that he wanted something different. It became the search for the ever-changing needle in the haystack—with no apparent solid reasons.

It isn't often that a recruiter walks away from a client they have been working with for years, but when others are hiring for all the right reasons and not wasting our time with BS, it makes sense. So, we fired them.

⬅➡

There are endless stories of hiring managers and companies similar to this. So many untrained hiring managers literally talk candidates out of the job. Can you imagine? Your company has been looking for the right candidate for months at who knows what cost, only to find out the hiring manager was talking each candidate out of the job.

One of the things we always do is fully debrief all candidates after the interview. This not only tells us how the interview went, but it gives us invaluable information about the hiring managers, the questions they ask, and details for future interviews.

This specific hiring manager, as it turned out, must have a big inferiority complex. The candidates we sent were all extremely qualified. In fact, he was scared they would be so good that he would lose his job. He would tell each candidate, "You don't want this job. The company doesn't give you the tools to succeed. My boss is a jerk." This went on and on. Finally, each candidate would come out of the interview saying they were no longer interested.

At first, you don't know what to believe. Was this just an opinion of the candidate? Or did they mishear these things? How could this be? So, after several interviews and taking good notes from our debriefs, we went to our client and told them what was going on. They were appalled. Imagine how many candidates they may have lost before we were called to help them.

They changed his responsibilities and wound up calling back several of the candidates and hired one of them.

Unfortunately, this is not a unique situation. We have run into so many hiring managers with these same issues. Instead of wanting strong candidates to help their department, realizing this will ultimately help them, they want weak candidates. They want folks who will get by but, more importantly, make them look better. Scary, huh?

⟵⟶

Another common scenario is companies that are afraid of making a hiring mistake. They want to see that perfect candidate with absolutely no faults or negatives, those who check off all the boxes in their job description. Who doesn't want that, right? Let's face it—those candidates are one in a million. There is always going to be one thing they don't have experience in. Or one area of weakness somewhere. That is just real life.

What these companies wind up doing is interviewing in the slim hope that they will find that one in a million. Doing so winds up costing a tremendous amount of time and money. So much so that some of these searches last years. All because the hiring manager or even someone in senior leadership is afraid to make the wrong choice and look bad to their superiors. But I would think taking a year to fill a position would make them look worse.

They start looking for any reason *not* to hire rather than all the reasons *to* hire. This goes on every day in the corporate world. Instead of seeing the candidates' verified accomplishments with people, dollars, technology, or whatever, they see the one weakness. Wouldn't it be more prudent to hire that tremendously qualified individual and train them?

I have seen hugely successful salespeople turned down because they hadn't sold one product out of the entire portfolio of products. Yet they have set records in sales for their current employer. Interestingly enough, that one product was 10 percent of the total.

I have always found that a star in sales can sell just about anything they believe in. The same can be said for that great engineer who may not have experience with one fraction of the machinery but is an expert in all other areas. Great engineers find a way to become knowledgeable in all aspects of their realm. Or the great research scientist who has all the qualifications and then some but lacks experience with one piece of equipment. Can't that skill easily be taught to a highly qualified scientist? I am told by experts that the answer is yes.

There are so many other examples of key issues—hiring managers who come across as dictators or don't even show up for the interview at all (even after the candidate has flown in from three states away).

Candidates constantly tell us that the hiring manager told them they had the job when, in fact, they don't. I assume it is because the hiring manager wanted to show their power. Perhaps it was to simply get out of the interview on a positive note. Whatever the reason, the candidate leaves thinking they have the job and instead get a rejection letter.

The same is true when hiring managers give out crazy salary numbers to candidates to impress them. Nothing will foul up an interview process faster than planting the seed of a salary that isn't realistic. That sets an expectation that simply can't be met. There is immediate disappointment and, of course, offer rejection.

We have seen hiring managers refuse to hire someone because they didn't go to the college they wanted, or they felt as though the candidate was too nice. They have chosen not to hire because they were too busy to bother with it all.

Many times, when a company is afraid of making a hiring decision, they will ask each candidate to take a series of tests.

Some are personality tests, some are technical, and others are a combination. There are so many varieties of personality tests out there that are being sold to "C" level managers as "foolproof." They are saying, "If you purchase our testing system, your hiring managers will have all the tools they need to avoid a bad hire." You would be surprised how often this happens. Who wouldn't want a foolproof option to avoid bad hires?

These tests can be great tools if used properly. If you use a personality test as a guide for areas where a candidate may need improvement or additional training, then it is being used correctly. If, however, it is being used as *the* tool for "hire/no hire" decisions, then it is going to lead to long-term complacency. The hiring managers will become complacent and lose their hiring skills completely. Why would they need to use judgment when their HR departments have given them a tool to keep them from ever making a mistake?

These tests, along with other things, can lead to paralysis by analysis. We have all heard that term, and it is often associated with all aspects of business and decision-making. There is no place where it is more evident than in the hiring process—when a company has had some bad hires, hires that have gone wrong for one reason or another. Companies start to question their hiring practices, and this will lead to paralysis. They will analyze every aspect of the candidate well beyond the reasonable.

What I find amusing is that it is often not the candidate at all. It is the hiring manager, departmental culture, lack of proper orientation, or any number of other things. You might think I am saying all this because I am a recruiter, and I have to defend my candidates. *No*! I am the first person to pull a candidate when we feel there is something wrong. I would never risk a relationship with a client over a bad candidate.

I am saying this because we are often given access to cultural issues and hiring manager issues that senior management may not see. How? Well, for one thing, many people in the corporate world are totally afraid of letting senior management see their internal department's cultural flaws. In some cases, they feel that would get them fired. However, they sometimes can't be hidden from the outside world regarding examples like that bad hiring manager. Or how a hiring manager treats their folks when everyone is afraid to speak up. I spent twenty-five years in the corporate world, and I saw this too many times. It is sad but true.

One of the largest issues facing the current market and hiring is the lack of urgency. Some companies take many months to make their hiring decisions. In today's market, that could drastically have a negative impact on your company. Nothing will kill a deal with a great candidate more than taking too long to make decisions. It is common for great candidates to often have four or five offers going at one time. In fact, that has become the norm. Being decisive and willing to step out on that proverbial limb is key. Often, the first offer is taken because candidates want to work for companies that are decisive. They know that if it takes months to make a hiring decision, that same issue is likely to plague them in getting things done within their own departments.

Life is a risk, right? So is hiring. A company often suffers more from that month's long lack of decision than they ever could from putting someone in who may need some training.

"Life is inherently risky. There is only one big risk you should avoid at all costs, and that is the risk of doing nothing."
—DENIS WAITLEY

"We cannot guarantee success, but we can guarantee failure merely by choosing not to try at all. Choosing to take a risk, however small, can have far-reaching implications in the course of human life."
—JOHN IZZO, PHD

"Learn from mistakes, yours and others. Do not let mistakes stop risk-taking! Identifying and evaluating risks are an integral part of our life."
—STEVEN ROSENTHAL

One of my biggest concerns with hiring companies is what I call "company arrogance." This phenomenon is prevalent in the corporate world. I totally understand where it comes from. It is rooted in the pride a person has in their job and their company. Company pride is a wonderful thing. I have had it most of my working life. I am very proud of the company I built from scratch. I was very proud of some of the corporations I worked for before that.

The difference is in the delivery. Exuding pride during your conversations with prospective candidates is a great thing. It immediately tells the candidate that you are not only happy with your job but happy with your company. However, don't let that pride spill over into arrogance. Don't come across like this company is so great . . . maybe you don't belong here.

Company arrogance is *real*. Hiring managers and even HR feel as though they do not have to sell their company's advantages to prospective candidates. That is simply not the case. In fact, in today's market, if you take that approach, you will be left out in the cold when it comes to top-tier talent. Successful hiring companies are selling what their companies can do for the candidates, not making them feel unworthy. No matter how much you may think there is no way this is happening, trust me, it is. Then, when the candidate turns down the offer, there is a total surprise. The hiring team will likely come up with excuses about the candidate rather than looking within.

All of these things I have mentioned are excuses not to hire.

"It is better to offer no excuse than a bad one."
—GEORGE WASHINGTON

*"I attribute my success to this:
I never gave or took an excuse."*
—FLORENCE NIGHTINGALE

*"He that is good for making excuses is seldom good
for anything else."*
—BENJAMIN FRANKLIN

I have mentioned some problems with hiring companies. Below is a summary of the largest areas of needed improvement for many hiring organizations:

DEVELOP SOLID HIRING PRACTICES FOR HIRING MANAGERS.
- Investigate best practices.
- Create a solid plan.
- Organize that plan to suit the various departmental needs.
- Be sure everyone is up to speed on company hiring objectives.

INTERVIEW TRAINING FOR ALL HIRING MANAGERS.
- Seek out in-depth training on interviewing skills.
- Institute a standard interview plan that best suits company needs.
- Remember, due to HR workload, they may not be the best source.
- Have hiring managers attend training and regular updates.

USE SOLID DECISION-MAKING TECHNIQUES.
- Trust your managers to make solid decisions.
- If you must test, use the testing to show areas of needed improvement, not hire/no-hire decisions.
- Use panel interviews wisely. Ensure the panel participants are solid decision-makers.

AVOID PARALYSIS BY ANALYSIS.
- Evaluate the overall skills of the candidates.
- Do not seek out reasons not to hire. Find reasons to hire.
- Stop overanalyzing the minutia.

MAKE TIMELY DECISIONS.
- Adapt to the speed of the marketplace.
- Develop expedited hiring plans for difficult positions.
- Be aware of the candidate's other opportunities.

MAKE GOOD OFFERS.
- Put your best foot forward first.
- Avoid lowball offers.
- Understand the market value of candidates.
- Be prepared to offer extras—sign-on bonuses, extra vacation, etc.

SELL YOUR ORGANIZATION.
- Sell the advantages of working at your company.
- Don't assume anything.
- Avoid company arrogance.

Having said all of that, there are many companies that do a solid job in their interviewing and hiring practices in general. Those that do have a process in place, and it works for them. There are so many things that come into play when searching for the next employee. There are several key areas that successful hiring companies explore in their interview process.

It would be impossible to list all the probable areas of interest for hiring companies here. In fact, I could fill a book on just that topic. However, most successful companies will use a set of basic interview topics. I will review those here, along with some typical questions within those topics. In addition to the ones listed here, there are hundreds of others.

BACKGROUND QUESTIONS
- Tell me about yourself.
- List your qualifications for this position.
- What are your greatest strengths?
- What are your greatest weaknesses?

PERSONALITY QUESTIONS
- What do you do in your spare time?
- What are your favorite hobbies?
- How would you describe your personality?

MOTIVE QUESTIONS
- How can you contribute to this company?
- Why do you want to work for this firm?
- Where do you hope to be in five years?
- What are your career goals?
- What is your biggest motivation?

JOB SATISFACTION QUESTIONS
- Why did you leave your previous employer?
- What did you like the least about your previous job?
- What did you like the most about that job?
- What are you looking for in your next job?

PAST PERFORMANCE QUESTIONS
- What type of decisions are most difficult for you?
- What causes you to become stressed?
- What are your greatest accomplishments?
- How would you describe your work ethic?

SALARY QUESTIONS
- What is your current salary?
- Are there other compensation factors (i.e., bonus, commission, etc.)?
- What salary are you looking for?
- What benefits do you have now, including vacation?

OTHER QUESTIONS
- Can you please provide us with three to five professional references?
- Are you willing to relocate?
- Do you mind if we verify employment, salary, etc.?

In addition to these basic questions and subjects, most successful companies will ask a series of behavior-based questions. These questions are intended to address various situations you have been confronted with and how you handled yourself in those situations. If a candidate's work experience is limited, such as a recent college graduate, these questions can also be used to get a glimpse of how the person might react to given scenarios.

Again, samples of behavioral-based interview questions are endless, but here are some commonly used questions:

- Describe a situation in which you were able to successfully persuade or convince someone to see your point of view.
- Describe a time when you faced a stressful situation that demonstrated your ability to cope.

- Give an example of a specific situation when your good judgment and logic solved a problem.
- Give an example of your setting a goal and achieving that goal.
- Tell me about a time when you had to present to a group.
- Tell me about a time when you had to go above and beyond the call of duty to get a job done.
- Tell me about a time when you had too much to do in a given period and how you were able to prioritize your tasks.
- Give an example of how you have motivated others.
- Tell me about a time you had to deal with a difficult coworker and how you handled it.
- Tell me about a time when you delegated a project effectively.
- Have you ever had to make an unpopular decision, and how did that go?
- Give an example of a project that required your organizational skills.
- Give an example of an innovative solution you came up with to solve a problem.

The list can go on and on. The real key here is to develop this line of questioning around those key topics that are critical to your open position and the department. These questions are ideal for digging into a person's traits, accomplishments, and personality by creating a need for them to give actual examples. I personally find these questions to be a better tool than personality tests. Many people simply do not test well but could clearly have great examples of the very things those tests try to analyze.

There are many other methodologies utilized by successful hiring companies. Going back to the basics, however, is always a good alternative. By that, I mean review and list the reasons the candidate is a fit. Then review and list the reasons the candidate is not a fit. The simple pros and cons list has been around forever. This is a great way to summarize the tools you have used as a final review of your candidate.

As I mentioned earlier, we always debrief the candidates after their interview to determine interest, fit, compatibility, issues, etc. We also debrief the clients or hiring companies after the interview. These debriefs are so important in determining if the interview went well, and they are also invaluable in determining the client's position on the candidate and the job. You would be shocked how often a company will change the position after an interview or series of interviews.

Candidates can open the company's eyes to the possibilities within a given position. Clients can suddenly realize the position has more depth than they realized. Or they may decide to alter the job description to add or delete requirements they initially thought they needed or didn't need. They may widen the search or narrow the search based on feedback from a candidate. In many cases, this is their first look at the view outside the company walls. This "outside look" may open their eyes.

This can be good or bad. Sometimes, it is good in that they realize they need to be a bit more forgiving of what they seek. They may realize that they were initially looking for a "needle in a haystack." In those cases, the search becomes more reasonable.

In some cases, however, they decide they want to add even more specifications to the job, making it more difficult to find. Those scenarios can become nightmare situations for the recruiter and, in many cases, the hiring manager. This can extend the search beyond the reasonable due to the added difficulty of more qualifications. Then the hiring manager suffers because they may desperately need to fill the position.

So, we debrief to get to the bottom of the results of the interview. Some of the questions we ask are

- Is this candidate the right fit for you?
- Do you believe the candidate can do this job?
- What do you consider their strong points?
- Any concerns raised during the interview?
- How was the chemistry?
- Was their personality a fit?
- Do you feel you can work well with this individual?
- What qualifications do you feel might be missing?
- What are the strengths and weaknesses of this candidate?
- Do you want to move to the next steps with this candidate?
- Where do they rank in comparison to other candidates?
- How do they compare to others within the organization?
- Do you want me to check references?
- Did you discuss compensation, and if so, how did that go?
- What else would you like for me to verify at this point?
- What do you see as the next steps?

Whether we ask these questions or you do, they need to be asked. Your ability to answer many of these questions will determine how sure you are about the candidate's fit for your position and company.

Step back and think about the reasons you need to fill the position. What key factors does this position bring to your organization? Does the person we just interviewed solve this need for the short term, long term, or even at all? How would they fit in with our culture? What do their references say about them?

There is an endless list of things to think about, but if you have done your homework and you have developed a clear hiring plan, it is simpler than many make it out to be. If you haven't developed a solid hiring plan and hiring process, *do so*. If you are not sure what you need, bring someone in who understands the current hiring market.

One of the biggest mistakes companies can make is not adapting their process to the current and ever-changing hiring market. What you did for the last ten years most likely will not work today. You need to have your finger on the pulse of what is going on in today's employment world. The things that were once selling points for your organization may not be today. Don't be afraid or hesitant to have someone look at your process to make sure it is appropriate for your next big hire.

MY HIRING PHILOSOPHY

I have hired hundreds of people in my career. Now that I am, let's say, getting "long in the tooth," I realize that those hires are one aspect of my business life that has brought me the most joy and fulfillment. I have grown to recognize what a tremendous feeling it has been to give so many people the opportunity to join organizations that I have been fortunate to be a part of.

Yes, my recruiting company has been responsible for getting thousands of people hired, and of course, that has brought me a great deal of joy. However, those personal hires, the ones I had the opportunity to work with in some way, have meant the world to me. Those are the folks I have gotten to know, learn about, learn from, help develop, watch grow, watch prosper, and see the results of their success and how it has impacted their lives and the lives of their families.

What more can you ask of your career than that?

We all hear and read about the people who run companies and how awfully they treat their employees. Heck, I know because I have seen it myself and, unfortunately, have been a part of that environment at one point in my career. We hear how greedy some managers are and how they hold people back for fear of their own careers. We hear how they can be abusive and mistreat others. How they can be discriminatory, and all the rest.

I believe that is a very small minority. Or at least that is my heartfelt hope. Those folks who do those things to their employees have missed out on the best part of business. My firm belief is this: *The best part of business is not your individual success. It is the success of others that you have played a part in.*

Along those lines, my words of wisdom on this topic are about what matters most in our lives. I presented this to my team, but it is just as important for family and friends and all of us.

LOOKING BACK
As time adds wisdom to our face,
We often look back to where we have been.
It is so much easier to do
Because it is what we know best.
When you take that look at paths crossed,
When you check all your mental notes,
When you think about the "wish I hads"
And wish I had nots,
When you look back at all the things that mattered . . .
What will have mattered more than
The people you have touched,
The memories you created?
What will matter more than
The tree you planted,
The smile you brought to that face,
The job well done?
What will matter more than
The hearts you crept into,
The children with whom you made a difference,
The folks that truly care about the walk you have taken?
Nothing will matter more than these.
So, as you look back,
Remember that your path today
Creates your look back for tomorrow.

MY HIRING PHILOSOPHY

Remember these things as you walk forward.
Remember to touch someone today.
Remember to make a difference in what you do.
Remember, because you always will.

I have had some hugely successful hires in my career. Of course, I have made some mistakes as well. After all, when hiring, you are dealing with human beings, and that can be an unpredictable exercise. But all in all, I have always had the good fortune of surrounding myself with wonderful, talented people.

When I was in the corporate world, I moved up the ladder to have my own departments. I know without a doubt that my growth in that world and my various promotions was due to those dedicated people on my teams. I tried very hard to treat everyone with respect and dignity and always did my best to make sure they had everything they needed to be successful.

One of the things I have always tried to do with every team I have managed over the years was to find a way for those teams to have fun. Yes, we were all totally dedicated to work and the company, but fun is critical for team unity, passion, and dedication. I would do that with various stories or jokes during a staff meeting. Or I would arrange an after-work happy hour. Sometimes, we would even do team events or trips. Because of the "fun" that we had in our groups, I was always able to recruit the best people. Lots of folks wanted to be in a department where there was fun in addition to work.

Now, don't get me wrong, I have always been a demanding boss. I always expected everyone's very best every day. I believe if you gave me your best, I would always give you my best. The best I offered was growth, rewards (financial and otherwise), recognition, and promotion opportunities.

The same was true when I decided to start my own business. I knew that I was getting into a world of unknowns. Lots of them. Anyone who has ever started a business knows there are a thousand things you don't know when you start. The one thing I did know was that I had to build an office culture that would enable me to hire well and, most importantly, retain my people.

The largest unspoken cost in the business world, in my opinion, is losing good people and having to train all over again and again. Turnover can kill a successful business faster than anything. Your people are your greatest asset. *Period.*

⇠⇢

As I was investigating how to start my own recruiting firm, turnover was the top issue facing recruiters. That was not going to be my fate. So, I developed a philosophy much like the one I had in the corporate world. We would have the things that make people want to work for me and *stay*.

I put together a plan for multiple goals—goals that are not "pie in the sky" but actually attainable by all employees. I created daily, weekly, monthly, quarterly, and annual goals. These were attached to the recruiting industry's notable gauges worldwide. Only we were going to stick to them.

We had call number goals for each period. We had "touch" goals, that is, the number of times you spoke to your candidates or clients depending on your role within the organization. We also sent candidate, job order, and placement goals. All of these are easily monitored and verified, and most importantly, all are easily reached if you follow our process.

Our process was that of a structured day to be able to cover the areas we needed in a given recruiting arena. I only mention this because it is important to note that goals don't mean anything if you don't give people a path and the tools they need to reach them. I repeat, *Goals don't mean anything if you don't give people a path and the tools they need to reach them.*

This is where I think the fun starts. Attached to each goal, we had several rewards. For example, for hitting two or three of your weekly target goals, you got to leave early on Fridays. That could range from an hour early to all day off, depending on the numbers you hit. Now, if you don't think that goal means anything to people, you are way off. That might have meant more to them than the financial goals . . . maybe! In any case, that is one goal that people would really strive for each week.

We had numerous financial goals. So much so that every employee, no matter their role, were on a bonus or commission plan. I won't go into the details of that plan here, but I will say that many recruiting companies have since adopted such a plan, and some have even copied mine exactly. An employee could double their salary with their various commission plans—and more often than not, they did just that.

The real problem with this job and all that I expected was that it takes a special kind of person. Many jobs do. I have managed a multitude of jobs over the last forty-five years, but I have not seen any that required more energy, dedication, commitment, and toughness than this one.

You see, in our job, you talk to people all day long. You either talk to candidates or you talk to prospective clients all day. Often, you hear the word "no" more than "yes." That same thing can be said about many sales-type jobs. Jobs where you are talking to people over and over who may not even know they need your services until you educate them.

Having seen the statistics of turnover in recruiting, I was naturally fearful of these issues. I felt as though I had set up a culture and a compensation plan, given all that I have mentioned above. But now I had to find the people who were willing to spend their day on the phone and be strong enough to handle the roller-coaster ride of emotions that go along with what we do.

I have seen so many suggestions on how to hire recruiters. I have been to seminars on that very subject. The seminar leaders would stand in front of the class, telling prospective recruiting managers what they look for in their employees. They would look for the usual things like education, sales experience, management experience, you name it. Yet, these were the very people who had had such struggles with turnover. In fact, at one of the sessions I was in, the leader had gone from forty-four recruiters (which is a huge staff in our industry) down to four when the economy turned bad. He was focused on IT recruiting, and as it often does, IT can turn sour in a given economy.

So, I asked him, "Since you have so many fully trained recruiters who you have invested so much time in, why didn't you shift with the market? Why didn't you put your best people on other industries that did not take that same downturn?" He said, "We are IT people, and that is what we will always be. IT recruiters can only recruit for IT jobs."

I thought this was the craziest thing I had ever heard. If you are good at something in your career and you need to shift to something else, chances are you can and will do that. Using the salesperson analogy, if you find a great salesperson who sells pumps and pump industry tanks, do you honestly not think that same person could sell something else? I sure do.

So, I started developing the list of things I needed to look for. I initially hired several people using those same skill sets everyone said I should look for. The right education, the sales experience, and all the rest. After a couple of hires that did not go well, I started to think back to all the people I had hired. What did the successful ones have in common?

ATTITUDE!

I am sure this is not a revelation to many of you. Many know this already. But I have found most who know it don't actually practice hiring that way. They still stick to those things they believe a person should have, just like they always did before.

I began searching for attitude, attitude, attitude!

I made the decision not to hire anyone with recruiting experience. I felt it was much harder to "unlearn" what they had been practicing than to learn my way of doing things. I felt the process we had developed was a great one, and from what I had seen in the marketplace, most recruiters were not dedicated to phones the way I felt they should be. Or they were not dedicated to "touches" the way I thought they should be. Former recruiters cringed when I told them about my expectations for phone work alone.

So, I had parents or friends of people start recommending their sons and daughters or friends getting ready to graduate college. They would ask me if I was hiring, and I would, of course, say yes. I would tell them to call me, and I would spend some time talking with them to see if this is something they might want to do.

I would ask questions about their interests, their passions, what motivates them, whether they are goal-oriented, etc. Then, I would ask them if they are motivated by money. Why? Remember, my goal structure was reward-based, so if money wasn't a motivator, they would not do well in this structure.

Many would give me the textbook answer when asked that question. You know, the answer their guidance counselor told them to say when asked the question. "Money is not the most important thing. Money is nice. Doing good things and helping people is my real motivation."

Don't get me wrong; those are wonderful things. Those are things that I try to do every day. So, I would say, "I get all that and understand that is how you were instructed to answer such a question, but what if I tell you that you can help people and make a *lot* of money at the same time? Now how does money fit as a motivator for you?" I could see the light bulb go on almost every time! When it didn't, I moved on.

The right attitude wasn't about the money they were going to make. It was about their willingness to see another approach, to be an open book and take a lot of guidance and constructive feedback. Were they willing to follow a process that just about guarantees success if you follow it? Would they be willing to ask a lot of questions and take a lot of feedback as they learned, with their ultimate goal being professional and financial success?

Many people will answer such questions the way they think you want to hear the answers. But if you watch and listen, you can tell who really means it. You can tell who gets excited about doing something new and different, along with being given the tools that make that possible. You can feel it in their answers and see it in their eyes.

I have since hired numerous people right out of college with those traits. Most have become hugely successful. They make lots of money and often have told me that they are making two to three times what their friends make that graduated with them. They have developed into top professionals within the company, have gone on to buy houses and multiple cars, and started families. All because they have the right attitude. An attitude of passion, dedication, and commitment. All because they want to do the right thing.

I have since used this same hiring pattern to hire people in their twenties all the way through to people in their seventies. Passion has no age limit. Attitude never has an age limit.

I have often told people I am interviewing that I have three requirements. They are simple and basic.

Be on time (a pet peeve of mine). In fact, I always say if you are not early, you are late.

Never lie (a major pet peeve of mine).

Always show respect to me and others (important in all aspects of life).

If you have all these things and show the right attitude every day, you can't help but be successful in whatever you do.

> *"Ability is what you are capable of doing.*
> *Motivation determines what you do.*
> *Attitude determines how well you do it."*
> —LOU HOLTZ

> *"Nothing can stop a man with the right mental attitude from achieving his goal; nothing on earth can help the man with the wrong mental attitude."*
> —THOMAS JEFFERSON

Now that I have discussed how I hire individuals for my company, the last topic regarding this matter is *teams*. Hiring good people is difficult to do. Hiring and developing a great team is even harder. One would conclude that hiring great people who fit the parameters I have laid out would easily evolve into a solid team. Most of the time, that is true. Unfortunately, there are situations where a person can fit what I and others look for—passion, honesty, commitment, etc.—but not be a good team player.

> *"Teamwork is the ability to work together toward a common vision. The ability to direct individual accomplishments toward organizational objectives. It is the fuel that allows common people to attain uncommon results."*
> —ANDREW CARNEGIE

> *"Alone we can do so little, together we can do so much."*
> —HELEN KELLER

> *"Talent wins games, but teamwork and intelligence win championships."*
> —MICHAEL JORDAN

In my opinion, teams don't evolve as a result of just having good people. Teams need to be developed. I strongly believe you have to work hard to develop the camaraderie, the willingness to help others, and the feeling of family, which is critical to the success of any team.

Family. Is the feeling of family really necessary to have a successful team? Maybe not in all businesses or groups, but in recruiting, it was absolutely vital to our success. Let me explain.

Recruiting, as I have described above, is a business unlike most others. There are constant rejections, and the need to overcome objections is a daily occurrence. There are certainly lots of victories and reasons to celebrate as well. The issue is, with the resulting roller coaster of emotion that exists in almost every recruiting firm, you need someone you can turn to constantly. That someone is your team family.

When that last-second rejection comes in when you were certain you were going to place a candidate, it can demoralize even the strongest person. The candidate changed their mind. Or they got that infamous counteroffer. Or the spouse decided, wait a minute, I am not moving away from my friends and family. Or the hiring company has a sudden downturn and freezes all hiring.

Whatever the reason, it hurts! It is gut-wrenching if you have put months into the project and did everything right. Who will understand the situation? Not your spouse or friends. They may sympathize with you but might never truly "get it." Why? Because they most likely don't experience this in their own jobs, or if they do, it is very seldom and probably not an immediate impact on their wallet. When this happens to a recruiter, they can see money, and sometimes lots of it, flying right out the window. In fact, in my early years of recruiting, when money was more critical, I would draw a picture of a $10,000 bill with wings on it and have it fly out the window.

Having said all of that, I believed that we needed to lean on each other. After all, we were the only ones who really understood that feeling to that degree. So, I put in place several things that I believe in that I think greatly contributed to the feeling of *family*.

> *"When everything goes to hell, the people who stand by you without flinching-they are your family."*
> —JIM BUTCHER

> *"A happy family is but an earlier heaven."*
> —GEORGE BERNARD SHAW

> *"Family is not an important thing. It's everything."*
> —MICHAEL J. FOX

The first thing I did was get everyone involved in training new people. Everyone would "shadow" a new person, review their duties, and walk them through their daily responsibilities. I had a consistent training schedule where everyone was responsible for teaching the new person something critical and, in some cases, numerous key functions.

The second thing I did was have regular meetings where everyone had the opportunity to speak to their week. There, they would go over things that had caused them difficulty. They were encouraged to bring in topics where they had made a mistake. They were asked to describe the mistake, how it happened, what could have prevented it, and lastly, what they will do differently next time.

Absolutely *no one* was criticized for mistakes. In fact, I always found mistakes to be a perfect scenario for training.

Another thing I did was implement weekly training on some topics of interest related to the job. Everyone had to take turns, and what they covered was up to them. In addition, each Friday during our weekly end-of-the-week staff meeting, a person was assigned to bring in "words of wisdom." These could be original (preferably) and motivational, as I have mentioned.

You would be shocked by how some folks really took to this. There were songs written, poems, general words of advice, and quotes from famous people. One person even did a rap about our job.

I know what some of you are thinking. *Man, this is corny stuff.* Well, think what you will, but it worked. We all shared each other's successes, each other's words (goofy or not), each other's training, and most importantly, each other's feelings. Isn't that what family is all about?

After a while, people really cared about each other. We knew some of their innermost thoughts. Some were very creative, and others not as much. But it didn't matter because no one was critical. Everyone was supportive. *Everyone.*

To add to the team feeling, I put in place some goals and rewards that we celebrated as a team and as a family. For example, when we hit a quarterly goal, we would shut down the office at noon the first Friday after the quarter, and we would hold Celebration Friday. We would go to some venue, often even to my home, and have food and drinks, talk, and have fun. Everyone loved hitting that quarterly target, getting together with each other, and not discussing work.

Isn't that what families do?

We had an annual goal for each person related to bringing in revenue. Every person had a target. If you hit that target, you won an all-expenses-paid trip for you and a guest to Las Vegas. Everyone that hit that would travel together. I put them up in one of the finest hotels, and we treated them to dinners, shows, and an all-around first-class time. It was a weeklong vacation. Talk about building camaraderie! Now, it was not just the team but also their significant other or best friend or whoever. They got to see what our company was all about. It was a vacation together.

Isn't that what families do?

Throughout these things, we have grown closer each year. We have basically demolished the "turnover expectation" of the recruiting industry. Most everyone stays. We still have my original hire, and our average tenure is well beyond any norm in the industry. We have numerous people with twenty, sixteen, fifteen years and growing. We pay very well, we work to help each other, we grow together, and we are everyone's second family.

Again, you may think some of these things sound goofy or corny. You may also think these things are expensive. They do cost money, for sure. But turnover, constant hiring, and constant training cost a great deal more. I am very proud of this group. I am proud of this philosophy. I am proud of this family.

SUMMATION

I started this book off by discussing how there could be unemployment in this great country of ours. Well, hopefully, you can see the many things that job seekers do and don't do that can cause unemployment. Whether it is the résumé's issues or the crazy interview scenarios, there are many reasons people don't get hired.

On the other hand, I tried to show some of the ways in which hiring managers miss out on hiring the best talent. These issues contribute greatly to unfilled positions across the country.

In addition to giving examples of how these things happen, I have shown the key things to do if you seek a job that will help get you noticed and hopefully find the position of your dreams. Conversely, I have tried to also show the things that Corporate America can do and frankly needs to do to hire the best candidates in the market today.

The topics discussed in this book are very important whether you are looking for your first job opportunity right out of college or your next career move. They are equally important to those seeking their last stop where they would like to finish out their career.

In my opinion, these topics are extremely critical to all those in the corporate world when trying to fill key positions. It doesn't matter if you are in human resources, the hiring manager, or the

CEO. All the points covered here can make a dramatic difference in your hiring process.

If you are a recruiter, then by all means, you need to take heed to these topics and these stories. Most of them you have lived yourself, and if you haven't, you surely will.

No matter which side you are coming from, the topics, key points, stories, and words of wisdom in this text can make a difference. I have tried to cover these things from all sides with the full intent of helping everyone. I know there are many who will think they don't need help and everything is working just fine. If it truly is, then I am extremely happy for you. However, if you see some of these points within your job search or key hiring needs, then it is all worth it.

The one thing I have learned is that I have a lot to learn. I have lived and breathed the hiring process truly from all sides for over forty-five years, and I can tell you that everyone can grow and learn about this always-changing phenomenon. It is, after all, about people. It is also about the times we live in. Lastly, it is about the world constantly changing.

Please take the time to listen, learn, and adapt. If you are a job seeker, then become a sponge and absorb everything you need to know about yourself and the job you seek.

If you are hiring, be open-minded and understand the market and perspectives of the ones you interview.

If you are recruiter, don't target the easy fit. Understand your client's needs and culture and do your best to fit those needs. The same goes for the candidates you represent and how you deal with them.

I truly wish you the best of luck in your search, your hire, or your placement. Remember to always treat others as you would want to be treated. If you live and work by that philosophy, you and everyone else will be in a better place.

ACKNOWLEDGMENTS

I would like to recognize all the folks I have worked with over the years. Especially to all of the staff of The Colonial Group, past and present, for their hard work and dedication.

I would like to thank all the HR managers I have worked with for their hard work, and I know you all have experienced many of the things covered in this book.

I would like to recognize and thank Management Recruiters International for their guidance in my early years of recruiting.

Thank you to all the companies I have worked with personally and those that my staff worked with for your professionalism.

www.ingramcontent.com/pod-product-compliance
Lightning Source LLC
LaVergne TN
LVHW041624070526
838199LV00052B/3234